Replenish The Earth
The Ministry Life Cycle

"Ministering with Purpose"
By

Dr. Laura Thompson

Copyright, 2009

AMC World, Inc.

First published 2009

Copyright © Dr. Laura Thompson 2009
ISBN #978-0-9720750-6-0

All rights reserved. Without limiting the rights under copyrights reserved above, no part of this publication may be reproduced, stored in or introduced into a retrieval system, or transmitted, in any form or by any means (electronic, mechanical, photocopying, recording or otherwise), without the prior written permission of the copyright owner.

Formatted using Open Office
Printed and bound in the United States of America
www.amc-world.com

Acknowledgments

I would first like to acknowledge God my creator who took the time to create me, not just once, but time and time again. He didn't just leave me spinning on the wheel. He molded me, and shaped me in a way so unique, that the gift he gave me could only fit in my vessel. If taken out and given to someone else, the gift would come as a sounding brass, a tinkling cymbal or an uncertain sound. My parents, Levi & Desrene Thompson have been at the core of my creative awareness. They never put a damper on the discovery of my intrinsic talents and abilities. Instead they encouraged me to pursue all that was in me. As a result, they were often shocked at the manifestation of things that emerged from this empty vessel. God can do anything.

While there are numerous mentors I'd like to thank (and they know who they are), I instead would like to give thanks to God for all of the trials, troubles and tribulations I encountered on this path. For without them I would not have a testimony. They served to test my character and the witness of the Holy Spirit within me. Today, I am the victor of my circumstances & experiences – not the victim.

I'd also like to extend special thanks to a dear friend who gave me the freedom to separate myself to God in order to produce this work. I really appreciate the sacrifice you've made during a very crucial time in your life and development. God who sees in secret will reward you openly.

I would also like to extend thanks and appreciation for the contributions made by Bishop Gladstone Royal, Mr. Floyd Muir of G & F Records, and Merlyn Ipinson Flemming of Emerge Me.

Replenish the Earth

The Ministry Life Cycle

By Dr. Laura A. Thompson

Table of Contents

Acknowledgments 3
Preface 9
Chapter 1 - The Invitation to the King's House 11
Chapter 2 - Walking in the Anointing 19
Chapter 3 - Conditions for the Invite 25
Chapter 4 - Being Anointed 29
Chapter 5 – Results: Ministry in Action 33

Preface

If ministry is indeed a life cycle, then it functions based on business and the principles of growth. The concept of cycles assumes that each stage can be perpetual/ongoing. Cycles continue over and over. The idea that life is a cycle denotes that it has a continuing growth factor. It is not possible to have life without creation and growth. After a person place or thing has reached a certain stage in development, a measure is assessed. In fact, measures are assessed throughout the process to determine normal and abnormal growth.

Most of what is written is based on the culmination of experiences and or observations made as people stepped into ministry. It is important to be intimately exposed to ministry behind the scenes. As you read of testimony and experiences both seen and felt, the intention is to introduce varying and sometimes narrow viewpoints, which will become cause in the matter of readers to take an introspective look at ministry within their own lives.

To minister is an act of the heart and comes from love and sacrifice for the betterment of people and for the fulfillment of purpose on the earth. Before one can get to "ministry" a link must be established between purpose and the gift(s). This book focuses a lot on gifts. I've been blessed with several gifts, which I choose to use for the purpose of building the kingdom of God. My heart is toward the souls of men and what can be done to restore those souls back to God – creator and giver of life.

Chapter 1 - The Invitation to the King's House

Selection/Rejection

I Samuel 16:23

This section is rather intriguing to me because it addresses a variety of hot topics including the anointing, jealousy, heart conditions, motivations and lots of other interesting subjects. After being in music and arts ministry for a number of years, an individual can attest to being the recipient or the victim of each one of these states of being. However the best premise to commence with is motivations.

Being Used and Being Used

A person's motives for being in ministry become increasingly exposed as they gain either more responsibilities or more notoriety. Like an individual who suddenly gains a large sum of money, personal habits and private motivations become intensified congruent to the amount of money received. For example, if a person is a natural giver, he or she will continue giving when more money comes into the picture.

Consequently, if one values clothing or alcohol while broke, when money arrives, these desires will be sought after in more creative and more luxurious ways. The principle is the same when it comes to the administering of gifts. To whom much is given, much is required. The parable of the talents comes to mind where the three servants were judged based on their innate motivations. When given the power and the resources to impact the world, what choices will be made? When someone provides a stage for the administration of a gift or talent, what's the first thing that comes to mind? Moreover, when the anointing of God showers down on individuals, how quickly do we move to the background, or at what point do we move to the lime light so the God takes center stage?

In theory, our motivation is God-ward, however in practice, all too often we find many functioning without the power. The good news (or not so good news) is that motivation is directly connected to what's going on in the heart. So in order to be in touch with motivation, one must be connected with his/her heart. Yes, the heart is an important organ in the body and in most cases is buried inside the chest cavity wall. In some cases, the heart is buried beneath much more than the chest's cavity wall.

The true intent of a person's heart can be buried behind

years of hurt, rejection, and jealousy, which can lead to hate, anger, resentment. Many like to roll these issues up into a 'package' known as emotional baggage. At times, people who identify with these and other issues are told to get over it and move on. All too often the person who's been bruised the most is the one that is called up to minister. Now, the calling to minister – be it in music, arts, drama, dance, etc. need not to be negated. It's just that this (ministering out of emotional baggage) is not the ideal scenario. This section of the book is for those bruised and battered vessels I'd like to call my "special pick."

In the Bible, there was a man named Saul who was anointed to be King of Israel. He was selected by the children of Israel and presented by God. One thing that is at times forgotten in this story is that this King was selected out of the condition of Israel's heart. Saul came on the scene after the period of the judges, where the general mindset of Israel was inward – introspective. While Saul started off pretty well as a leader, he fumbled miserably due to the condition of his heart, which by the way, was a mere representation of state of Israel.

Saul was anointed in the beginning. Being anointed gives an individual and air of confidence that God is with them. However, there is a distinct difference between "God is with me" and "I got this". The former represents complete reliance on the giver of gifts, while the latter symbolizes reliance on a move and a movement that has passed. It also assumes that God will move the same way all the time and/or the real anointing comes from the gift, not the creator and grantor of the gift. And while the gifts and callings of God are without repentance, both must be submitted to the will of God at all times in order to have any affect on the environment or the situation that calls for the gift's administration. In general, people who consciously choose to function in the anointing get consistent results.

This leads us to a discussion on the invitation. Many in ministry become really excited when they get an invitation. Just think of it. You've been consistent in serving (or not). To some, the invitation represents an opportunity – a step up. The invitation shows that some one wants you. And by using these descriptions, the invitation really represents a deep seeded heart condition, which if left unresolved could fester. This is why internal motivation must be taken into account at the receipt of an invitation to sing, to dance, to preach, to play music, etc. What's being serviced at the acceptance of an invitation? If one's pride is being satisfied, or if the air of rejection has been lifted as a result of the invitation, then it's possible that the real purpose of the invitation was for you to check the intent of you heart and address the unresolved motivational factors.

The truth of the matter is that invitations to minister may not come at the most convenient times. Further, the person inviting you may not be all that thrilled to extend an invitation, nor will he or she be eager to serve you during your tenure. However, if you're on divine assignment, then the purpose of your mission cannot be aborted. Some invitations to help come as a result of jealousy, intense pain, and anguish. Just think your typical doctor visit. In the case of an unhealthy person, a doctor is invited to correct behavior leading to the unhealthy lifestyle. If the unhealthy individual is content to live a mere existence of his/her life, the doctor's invitation won't come without resistance. Regardless, the doctor is there to restore as much balance and he or she can with the time and resources available. Even prophets in scripture came into situations to restore things that had gotten off course. The point is that just because you're the person chosen for the hour to minister, does not automatically equate to "everyone is so happy that you arrived."

When ministering, it's important to think past the opportunity and look towards the intended purpose of your gift and God's working power. It's during the development stage that individuals need to experience the varying applications of the gift. Performance is only one very small aspect of stirring the gift. When coupled with the order of the word of God, the administration of the gift will function to reprove, rebuke, correct or instruct.

This brings us to verse 23 of the story of King Saul. Here, Saul is rejected. He functioned outside of the anointing. Instead of relying on God's power, Saul consults a witch in efforts to exercise a power that did not originate from him. The anointing of God cannot be contained in human hands or mimicked by sorcery. A true anointing removes burdens and destroys yokes. Further, the anointing is not restricted to an individual's stature, because indeed man looks at the outward appearance, but God looks at the heart (verse 7).

Your next invitation could be to a place where God's anointing is not. This is the point where the performers step aside and the anointed arise to the fulfillment of purpose. I strongly suggest you go anointed and appointed in fulfillment of the divine order. This was the case with David. He had an invitation by King Saul, an appointment by God, a charge to keep and a God to glorify. Also note, that in the administration of your gift, you may not utter a word to the intended audience. When that is the case, take on the possibility that it is the way you serve that is a louder witness than anything words could say at that time. Through a humble and contrite heart, a dancer could be administering the strongest rebuke that could be given at that time. There is no limit to God's power and there is no substitute for his anointing on any situation.

ASSESSMENT/STUDY QUESTIONS:
1. List five key points from this chapter.
2. What does this chapter reveal to you about God's power?
3. What from this chapter can you apply to your ministry/calling in music and arts?
4. How can the principles from this chapter apply to your life?

Chapter 2 - Walking in the Anointing

So you say you want to walk in the anointing until people see and experience that you are anointed. Your desire is that when you enter the room that even the demonic host knows who you are. This request is not just a name drop or a popularity contest. And while we read of he many heroics of people the Bible, with those triumphs came a series of trials each went through in pursuit of the prize of the high calling of God in Christ Jesus.

Trials test character and motives. How an individual goes through directly point to the fruit of the Spirit within that man or woman. Varying degrees pressure, press out every idol and doubt. The experience of the press produces testimony, which can only be given by a testator – one who has been tried and come <u>through</u> the other side.

Some want the anointing so they can be known for the tricks they can perform. There are four young men in the Old Testament that were part of the same Levitical lineage. Two of the young men, Nadab and Abihu, were Aaron's sons. They ended up producing strange fire and eventually where killed

(Leviticus 10). The other two young men were sons of Eli, Hophni and Phinehas. Eli chose to honor his sons above the statutes and principles of God. Both sons were killed during a battle and Eli died soon after.

One thing that is ironic about this story is that many scholars indicate Eli as the grandson or Aaron, (son of Ithamar). Ithamar was the brother of Nadab and Abihu. Also note that when Moses went to the mountain to seek God, Aaron participated in the creation of an idol for worship. Faithful worship has been under siege in this family since the time Aaron assisted in building the golden calf (Exodus 32: 1 – 3). Put another way, somehow, this family failed to properly denounce inappropriate worship to God. This generational issue followed this family in scripture, until God was fed up. Throughout the generations, we find examples where they added something that did not belong to the worship. Authentic anointing from God cannot come as a result of strange fires, the erecting of idols and sexual impurity.

It was even more crucial for this group of people who came from the tribe of Levi (the Levitical Priesthood). These men were supposed to usher people into worshiping God. Instead, they participated in leading people away by adding something man made to the worship. God's glory cannot be shared with another. God permanently removed this line of

Levites from priest duties. Instead of Phineas taking on the mantle of his father, he and his brother were killed and Samuel became the next judge and prophet of Israel.

Thus while one's desire to be of service may be admirable, the motives behind the service makes the vessel honorable or dishonorable. We see this in many instances, where individuals provide a service for the person or king in charge, as men pleasers. But the condition of the heart does not match the service provided. What do you really want & why are you following so hard after it?

Acts 16:16-18 speaks of a young girl who followed hard after Paul and Silas. She proclaimed the truth – that they were servants of the Most High God (Acts 16:17). However, being fortune-teller, her motives were demonically charged. The Spirit within her knew that Paul and Silas possessed the Spirit of God. She was definitely a man pleaser motivated by the money she was being paid to provide divinations for her masters who enslaved her. The anointing of God provides power for service – enabling people to be empowered, not entrapped or enslaved. Paul eventually rebuked the spirit that was influencing this slave girl.

The word of God is "profitable for doctrine, for reproof, for correction, for instruction in righteousness" (2 Timothy 3:16). If a person wants to walk in the anointing, he/she will need to have directions. A person must be in a position to receive direction in the form of doctrine, reproof, correction and instruction in order to be lead/directed by the Spirit. . If an individual is incapable of being corrected, and reproved or fails to receive instruction and is in rebellion to doctrine, then what spirit will this individual be led by?

Sometimes people can become too familiar with the works and the miracle that they forget to seek God for divine favor and direction. People, who know where to go fail to ask for directions. Walking in the anointing means giving up your ideas on where you think you should go or how you think things should go, and asking God for direction.

Samuel's servant heart and humility enabled him to be God's choice to serve Israel after Eli. A servant's heart says, speak Lord for thy servant hears (I Samuel 3:10). The heart of a servant honors the words of the Lord, not letting any fall to the ground (1 Samuel 3:19, KJV). According to the Message version of this text, Samuel's prophetic record was flawless.

It was during Samuel's reign as the prophet of Israel that Saul was selected as king, but was eventually rejected by God because he rebelled against God's word (1 Samuel 15: 22 – 23). While walking and doing, ministers can become disconnected from the cause, the passion and the creator of the ministry. They just have a ministerial walk or they are caught up in doing the work of ministry.

They remind me of the 1955 movie starring James Dean, entitled "Rebel Without A Cause" (Ray, 1955). The movie, directed by Nicholas Ray was about a rebellious teenager. However the movie spawned from a documented 1944 case study by Dr. Robert Linder entitled, *Rebel Without a Cause: The Hypo analysis of a Criminal Psychopath* (http://en.wikipedia.org/wiki/Rebel_Without_a_Cause). Ministries, businesses, marriages and the like who are caught up in doing the work without being connected to the source, appear listless – walking around and with the performance of zombies. In other words, it is possible to being walking a carrying out the work of a business, a marriage and or a ministry while being in a state of disconnect.

Thankfully, this was not the case with David. Then David was selected and known as a man after God's heart (1 Samuel 15:26). David sought after the heart of God in all matters of life and ministry. The works of David are recording in the New Testament, where he's known for doing everything God told him to do (Acts 13:22, NIV). David had his flaws as many of us do; however, his heart was pliable toward the will of God and his work. As a result, the word of God became profitable to David for doctrine, reproof, correction and instruction. A vessel that is willing and obedient can be used again and again in a wide variety of environments.

ASSESSMENT/STUDY QUESTIONS:

1. List five key points from this chapter.
2. What does this chapter reveal to you about God's power
3. What from this chapter can you apply to your ministry/calling in music and arts?
4. How can the principles from this chapter apply to your life?

Chapter 3 - Conditions for the Invite

Imagine . . . you've attended the Wednesday evening session of a revival. The speaker called you out of the audience. Through the prophetic anointing, the speaker told you that you were anointed of God, and that you would begin to minister people in high places. Weeks later you look at yourself in the mirror and see that you were doing the same thing you've been doing last month. What happened? Was the speaker incorrect? Did you do something wrong? Has God changed his mind? Through a brief perspective of the selection process and David's example, we will discover the answers to these questions.

The scenario described above is one that I can relate to. At certain times, the Lord would use his vessel in varying capacities like singing, speaking, dancing, acting, interpreting dreams, etc. Sometimes people in the audience are extremely shocked, amazed, emotionally charged, extremely encouraged or just plain 'ole blessed and inspired by the way the Lord used his vessel. Then someone in the crowd approaches with what they call a word from the Lord.

Truthfully, some of the comments are just that – a comment or compliment coming across as some divine impartation. Some comments are blessing towards you and your ministry with a prayer of encouragement that you'd continue. Through the confirmation of the Spirit and signs following, people inspired by the Spirit pronounce blessings as well, but overall nothing is said that has not been said before. The word spoken was so general that anyone could have gotten up and received it as a word for them. Nothing said resembles the impartation bestowed on David by Samuel.

Then, when you least expect it, a man or woman of God comes to you, prays over you, and at an opportune time speaks a word over your life, which aligns with who you are, where you are, and to whom you are going to reach. The word confirms the petitions made in the stages of development. Your role and your calling are clearly identified and confirmed through the word of God in this message.

There is clearly a difference between a compliment, a blessing, an encouragement, and a prophetic word. People truly anointed by God receive their share of each (as seen above). The mistake that's often made is where some choose to move into ministry as a result of numerous compliments, blessings and encouragement. Inspired by what was said, he/she constantly looks for more compliments and encouragement and more blessings to keep going. Of course when compliments, encouragement and blessings don't come, he/she becomes discouraged and their ministry tends to reach an abrupt halt. Surely, people in ministry need as much encouragement, as they can get. As we'll see through the life of David, this is clearly not enough to sustain an individual throughout their life cycle in ministry.

ASSESSMENT/STUDY QUESTIONS:
1. List five key points from this chapter.
2. What does this chapter reveal to you about God's power?
3. What from this chapter can you apply to your ministry/calling in music and arts?
4. How can the principles from this chapter apply to your life?

Chapter 4 - Being Anointed

God instructed Samuel to go to Jesse's house to anoint the next King of Israel (1 Samuel 16). Jesse shows up with seven sons, none of whom are selected. The eighth son, who was eventually selected, was already in the field working – not at the sacrifice. Unlike his brothers, externally, this son (David) didn't look like a king, but was selected based on the condition of his heart.

After the anointing by the prophet, David goes back into the field. He did not stop doing what he had always been doing. He didn't wait for Saul to die. He did all he knew to do for his father's house and the sheep of his field. The point here is that after the acknowledgment of your gift, calling and appointment, it's not time for you to just sit around waiting for someone to die. Get back to work.

While out in the field, David earned a reputation as a skilled musician. In other words, no one called on him to do what David was already doing. So if no one calls on you to do anything for a while, it doesn't mean that you're not gifted or you're not able to minister. If no one appears to notice you for several years, be like David and play, preach, sing, and dance in front of a heavenly audience. David played in the field. Who knows the number of animals that could testify of his skill and ability?

A ministry that is based on the acknowledgment coming from people won't last for long. People come and people go. Sometimes they're with you and sometimes they're with someone else. Also note that creatively reinterpreting God's plans won't get you to your destiny any sooner than with God's original timing. (Remember Abraham and Sarah – Genesis 16). When the time was right, God blessed Sarah and Abraham with their own child in their old age. When the time was right, God enabled David's musical gift to make room for him.

David received an invitation to play for King Saul at the King's palace. While he knew the king's throne was his destiny, David respected the office and did the work he was assigned to do. Upon receiving the invitation, it's important to note that no one will be training you. When you are called you must be ready to give an answer to the hope of your calling (Ephesians1:18).

In most cases, there will be no entourage parading around you. Like a substitute teacher, your intended audience may not really want you to be there. They may have a preference for someone else to be in your shoes to entertain or minister to them. At one point, King Saul almost killed David with a javelin. Whether or not he was liked or appreciated by Saul, David was still God's chosen vessel.

The condition of the vessel may not be conducive to what one envisions a vessel to look like. The vessel may seem frail to the onlooker. The capabilities of the vessel appear bleak in the eyes of some. Regardless of what it looks like, given the opportunity, the vessel must do what it was intrinsically designed to do. Moreover, it is expected that given the opportunity that you (like David) know what to do with or without supervision.

ASSESSMENT/STUDY QUESTIONS:
1. List five key points from this chapter.
2. What does this chapter reveal to you about God's power?
3. What from this chapter can you apply to your ministry/calling in music and arts?
4. How can the principles from this chapter apply to your life?

Chapter 5 – Results: Ministry in Action

Reproduction, Replication, Replenish
Reproduction is the process of creating something that was already created (duplication based on an earlier version of something).

Replication is the process of repeating, duplicating or reproducing something. Many are on the quest to reproduce or replicate themselves in others. Consequently, it's not that difficult to create a copy or most anything whether good or bad. People are willing to follow after anything that's going somewhere or doing something...some cause or military command. However, reproduction and replication do not always equate to replenishment.

Replenishment means to restock depleted items or material or to fill somebody with needed energy or nourishment. According to the command of God from creation, we are commanded to be fruitful, multiply and replenish the earth (Genesis 1:22). Being the salt of the earth, by nature what we produce has the ability to not only cause others to follow in the example set, but to also provide nourishment and to restock in the areas of the earth where there's lack and insufficiency. As mentioned earlier, where there is no soul prosperity there can be no spiritual replication that replenishes the earth. With this comes the disclaimer that some attempt to reproduce from the condition (mess) they are in. And thus, they are successful replicating that condition (mess) in abundance. This could explain why some plans toward growth steadily go into decline before they decline prematurely.

There are numerous ways to be reproductive in ministry. Examples include (but are not limited to) providing recordings of your sermons or workshops, teaching, writing literature or music, etc. In other words, people need to have access to something you've said or done beyond you. Your presence is limited by location, in that you can only be at one location physically. If something about your ministry is noteworthy, then provide a means by which people can have access, at their leisure and convenience.

In fact, I am of the strong opinion that today's minister should not minister unless they have product available somewhere (whether tangible, e.g. CD, book, workshop notes, etc.; or intangible, e.g. electronic version, Internet based, etc). It's always great seeing someone live or hearing someone do a live broadcast. But with the age of digital television, (where people can rewind portions of a missed broadcast), fused with internet broadcasting, there's no need to provide your audience with inconvenience by not using the technology to create a product.

There are quite a few rules and regulations associated with administering copies of your product, especially if that product is for an online audience. I will deal with some of the main issues in the upcoming section on Ministry Outside the Gate. The main point here is that reproduction and replication can eventually lead to replenishing the earth.

People lacking the skills and ability to reproduce can be stuck at this level in their ministry life cycle. As mentioned earlier, graves are full of unrealized potential. In some cases, being stuck here is worse for the person who is alive and cannot bring his/her ministry to the next level that it reproduces in others. At a certain age/stage in a person's life reproduction is a necessity. The proverbial "biological clock" begins to tick internally. Thoughts of legacy begin to plague the mind. Certainly there must be someone who can benefit from your life and the gifts you've been given. Someone must be edified by your life and your testimony.

Ministry in Action

As more people and communities become edified by the gift(s), your testimony then becomes your reputation of consistency in ministry. People that are consistent in delivery are seen as being results oriented. You may know someone that actualizes everything she says. Or whenever certain man prays on your behalf or on the behalf of others, the prayer is answered.

Soon after, people begin to know of your talent. You can be counted on as a vessel that maintains the same level of consistency when used. If this were a course in marketing, your talent would be the equivalent of your Brand. Then people begin to boast or testify (Promote) of what they've seen or experienced from your gift. Suddenly your gifts and abilities are being recommended to key decision makers in society.

Arioch, the captain of the King's guard, recommended Daniel to King Nebuchadnezzar (Daniel 2:14 & 15). The chief butler recommended Joseph as one who could interpret Pharaoh's dream (Genesis 41: 9 - 14). In 1 Samuel 16:23, the king's servant recommended David as one who could help King Saul. By the time these young men were recommended to the kings they served; a level of quality was developed and maintained, that could be produced time and time again. The gift made room for them- establishing a home base for their operation in the King's palace. Each was divinely positioned and part of an influential network of people who knew their reputation. And none of this would have occurred without constant prayer, the divine connection with God, which had been developed in the dark places. As you stay in the anointing and under God's divine control, the Lord will reposition you to fulfill His purpose.

Invitation and Purpose

Some invitations are less welcoming than others. A reprise to this section is almost like several verses of a song, sung by David himself. It goes a bit like this:

> Deliver me from my enemies, O God; protect me from those who rise up against me. Deliver me from evildoers and save me from bloodthirsty men. (Psalm 59:1 & 2 NIV)

> My times are in your hands; deliver me from my enemies and from those who pursue me. (Psalm 31:15 NIV)

> Rescue me from the mire, do not let me sink; deliver me from those who hate me, from the deep waters. (Psalm

69:14 NIV)

Could this be the end result of an invitation? At first glance the words from these songs by David may invite a person to stay at home under the covers until it looks safe to come out. The truth of the matter is that it is possible that a divine invitation could lead to a request for deliverance from God Himself. The good news is that there is nothing to be alarmed about.

If God sets up appointments for you to minister, then His deliverance and his divine providence is included in the package. In fact, his protection was included before the invitation was accepted. What a mighty God we serve! I'm reminded of military personnel that serve our nations. They have a promise of national protection under varying circumstances. However even that promise has its limitations. If the nations' armed forces and militia are in service to protect its citizens, who is protecting them? Only when individuals are fulfilling divine appointments in response to a higher calling can they sing,

"My hope is built on nothing less than Jesus blood and righteousness. I dare not trust the sweetest frame but wholly lean on Jesus name. When darkness seems to hide His face, I rest on His unchanging grace. In every high and stormy gale, my anchor holds within the veil. On Christ the solid rock I stand all other ground is sinking sand..."(Bradbury & Mote, http://www.worshiparchive.com/worship_chord_sheet.asp?t=song&id=143).

As I watch the City Games in Manchester, England, I'm reminded of the training an athlete goes through prior to a race. A change of diet, endurance running, timed running, and weight training are just a few of the things that are required to condition the body for the big test. Good trainers place their athletes in various environmental scenarios in efforts to break down their resistance to change.

During this race in Manchester, the track was wet due to rainy conditions. Yet the runners ran despite the rain and the puddles on the track. With great concentration, one of the runners even broke the world record, which he set a year prior. An opportunity was also created for the other runners. They benefited by measuring how close or far away they were in their training from the fastest man in the world – still well worth the trip.

Consequently, the point of this story is to emphasize that people need to work in areas that maximize their training. Training in ministry occurs in the field of testing. Invitations that don't test your gifting do not provide the opportunity for you to minister. For example, if you received substantial training/testing to discern evil spirits, yet you are working in the laundry room, then your gifting is not being maximized.

Planning & Effectiveness

There is a famous quotation that says those that fail to plan, plan to fail. As the focus changes and the goals are accomplished, it becomes important for organizations to make changes and plan for additional growth. The organization or lack of organization of any department will determine its effectiveness. Many of the kings of the Old Testament scripture created strategies to combat and defeat their enemies. Those that did not plan an effective strategy realized very quickly that they were on the road to defeat.

This application is very essential to plan of attack when dealing with spiritual warfare. In essence, praise and worship invokes the presence of the lord and dismisses the assignment of the enemy of our souls. But the attack must be a direct hit – not a near miss or fumble. In order for this to be accomplished, an organized set of functions must be in place. One of the most logical places for the departments' functions to be listed is within their mission, objective and vision statements. After the overall functions have been set, an additional list of plans and schedules needs to be set aside for each service.

Let us take for example, the Sunday morning worship

service. Depending on how your church organization is set up, the person in charge of devotion, the choir and thus the music director and musicians need to know the overall theme of the service. This theme usually comes from either the Pastor or the Auxiliary director in charge of the morning service. Depending on the number of people involved in music, adequate time in preparation and planning is essential for many reasons.

First, when there is a theme, songs and scripture can be selected to engulf that central thought –thereby penetrating the hearts and mind of the congregation. As a result, the minister will not have to toil as hard to get his message across to the listeners, nor will he or she have to perform tricks (like telling stories or jokes) to keep the audience focused on the subject matter. Why? It is because they've been exposed to it throughout the entire service – or at least for the moments leading up to the message. The Mission and Objective from the pastor becomes the overriding mission and objective of each person involved during the Sunday service. As a result, the objective of every person (from the usher to the trumpet player) becomes aligned with the pastor's vision.

This is important because, the enemy spends lots of time and energy on trying to get the audience focused on everything else but the word of God during the message. Getting the hearts and minds of the congregation focused on the word is a significant blow to the enemy of our souls.

Manifestation from the Spirit of truth is what the world is crying out for. The Spirit of the Lord is just waiting for his people to get themselves together to spread his glory throughout the earth. And this goal can be accomplished in a congregation when people are aligned with one common goal and working with one vision.

Many of the things discussed in the book thus far have been based on ministries within an existing structure. The examples and themes from the main patriarchs of the Bible relating to this subject matter (David, Joseph, Daniel) were all promoted to work in major roles in society under to rule of the King of their day. My desire is for the readers of this book to strive to become influential members of society while in pursuit of your ministry. God can and will position his chosen vessels any and everywhere to manifest his glory throughout the earth. The upcoming section will present a few basic business and industry principles that are relevant for ministries that function outside of an organization or governing system.

ASSESSMENT/STUDY QUESTIONS:

1. List five key points from this chapter.
2. What does this chapter reveal to you about God's power?
3. What from this chapter can you apply to your ministry/calling in music and arts?
4. How can the principles from this chapter apply to your life?